MAX LUCADO

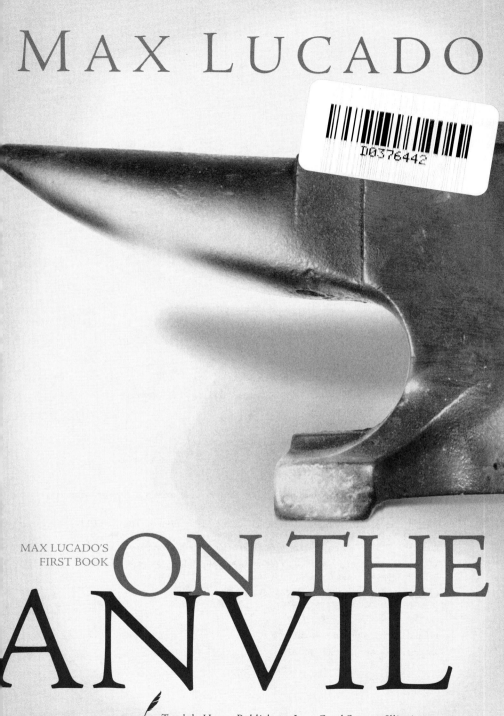

MAX LUCADO'S
FIRST BOOK

ON THE ANVIL

Tyndale House Publishers, Inc., Carol Stream, Illinois

Visit Tyndale's exciting Web site at www.tyndale.com

TYNDALE and Tyndale's quill logo are registered trademarks of Tyndale House Publishers, Inc.

On the Anvil

Designed by Jacqueline Nuñez

Library of Congress Catalog Card Number 85-50732
  ISBN-13: 978-1-4143-1553-9 (sc)
  ISBN-10: 1-4143-1553-8 (sc)

Printed in the United States of America

14   13   12   11   10   09   08
7   6   5   4   3   2   1

TO MY MOTHER AND FATHER,
two people with the courage of a giant,
and the heart of a child.

TABLE OF
CONTENTS

ACKNOWLEDGMENTS

With tenderest appreciation to
Doug and Carl—
for three unforgettable Gold Coast years.

Stanley, Landon, and Lynn—
for helping the Word become an action verb.

Steve and Cheryl—
for your unquenchable loyalty.

Fern, Sue, and Laurie—
for keeping your eyes on my grammar
and your fingers on the typewriter.

And, most of all, to my lifelong partner, Denalyn.
If every man had a wife like you,
how sweet the world would be!

FOREWORD

Flipping through the pages of this book brings a flood of memories of where I was when the words were written. Most of the pieces were composed when I was an associate minister of a downtown church in Miami, Florida, years ago. One of my tasks was to write a weekly article for the church bulletin. Many ministers dread such tedium. But I grew to relish the task. Because I was single at the time, I stayed in my office until late at night, writing and rewriting the pieces. The bulletin was small, so my essays were brief. I had no thought that the articles would ever be read outside of the church, which explains why many of the illustrations are local. But the pieces were read outside of Miami. I began receiving letters from people around the country requesting copies of the articles. For the first time, I was exposed to the power of the written word. The pen, I realized, would speak to people I did not know, in places I might never go, in ways I otherwise never could.

I was amazed.

Then I received a letter from Randy Mayeux, a friend who at that time lived on the West Coast. "You should consider writing for publication," he said. I thanked him, filed the letter away, and didn't give the idea much thought. It wasn't that I wasn't interested. I just didn't have the time. I was busy preparing for my wedding and a move to Brazil. Where would

I find time to rework the articles, compile them in a book, and mail them to publishers?

The answer? I found the time in Brazil. When Denalyn and I moved to Rio de Janeiro in 1983, we spent several hours a day in language study. During the evenings I wrote. I spent several weeks rewriting the articles and weaving them into a manuscript. Not knowing the name of a single publisher, I went into my library and copied the addresses of fifteen publishing houses and mailed them all a copy.

Six sent it back unopened. Six opened it, but said "no, thanks." Three expressed an interest, and one of those three, Tyndale House, sent me a contract. I was stunned. I will forever be grateful to Dr. Wendell Hawley and the Tyndale family for taking a risk on me and publishing my first book.

On the Anvil predates many better-known efforts such as *No Wonder They Call Him the Savior, Traveling Light,* and *3:16: The Numbers of Hope.* It's the only book I wrote when I was single. In fact, it's the only book I wrote before I had children. If I remember correctly, I received the contract the same day Denalyn and I received news of her first pregnancy.

It is also the only book of mine my father ever saw. He died soon after its initial publication.

I never dreamed of being an author. Never. The words in the book are not those of an aspiring penman. As you read *On the Anvil,* you are reading the thoughts of a young missionary writing from his soul. The style isn't as good as it should be. Some of the pieces are too abrupt, others are too wordy—but it's my first book, and it has a special place in my heart. I wouldn't change a single word of it.

Thanks again to Tyndale for taking the chance. Thanks to Dr. Wendell Hawley and Mark Carpenter for seeing the potential. And thanks to you for picking up this edition of *On the Anvil.*

— Max Lucado

THE BLACKSMITH'S SHOP

In the shop of a blacksmith, there are three types of tools.
There are tools on the junk pile:
> *outdated,*
>> *broken,*
>>> *dull,*
>>>> *rusty.*

They sit in the cobwebbed corner, useless to their master,
oblivious to their calling.

There are tools on the anvil:
> *melted down,*
>> *molten hot,*
>>> *moldable,*
>>>> *changeable.*

They lie on the anvil, being shaped by their master, accepting
their calling.

There are tools of usefulness:
> *sharpened,*
>> *primed,*
>>> *defined,*
>>>> *mobile.*

They lie ready in the blacksmith's tool chest, available to their
master, fulfilling their calling.

Some people lie useless:
> *lives broken,*
>> *talents wasting,*
>>> *fires quenched,*
>>>> *dreams dashed.*

They are tossed in with the scrap iron, in desperate need of repair, with no notion of purpose.

Others lie on the anvil:
> *hearts open,*
>> *hungry to change,*
>>> *wounds healing,*
>>>> *visions clearing.*

They welcome the painful pounding of the blacksmith's hammer, longing to be rebuilt, begging to be called.

Others lie in their Master's hands:
> *well tuned,*
>> *uncompromising,*
>>> *polished,*
>>>> *productive.*

They respond to their Master's forearm, demanding nothing, surrendering all.

We are all somewhere in the blacksmith's shop. We are either on the scrap pile, in the Master's hands on the anvil, or in the tool chest. (Some of us have been in all three.)

In this collection of writings, we'll take a tour of the "shop." We'll examine all tools and look in all corners. From the shelves to the workbench, from the water to the fire . . .

And I'm sure that somewhere you'll see yourself.

We'll discover what Paul meant when he spoke of becoming "an instrument for noble purposes." And what a becoming it is! The rubbish pile of broken tools, the anvil of recasting, the hands of the Master—it's a simultaneously joyful and painful voyage.

And for you who make the journey—who leave the heap and enter the fire, dare to be pounded on God's anvil, and doggedly seek to discover your own purpose—take courage, for you await the privilege of being called "God's chosen instruments."

PART ONE
THE PILE OF
BROKEN TOOLS

1
THE PILE OF
BROKEN TOOLS

To find me, look over in the corner of the shop,
   over here,
      behind the cobwebs,
         beneath the dust,
            in the darkness.
There are scores of us,
   broken handles,
      dulled blades,
         cracked iron.
Some of us were useful once, and then . . . many of us never
   were.
But, listen, don't feel sorry for me.
Life ain't so bad here in the pile . . .
   no work,
      no anvils,
         no pain,
            no sharpening,
And yet, the days are very long.

Are you broken, too?

Do you think God might be calling you "off the pile"? What would that require of you?

2
I AM VERY
WEARY

It will be remembered as one of the most confounding missing-persons cases.

In August 1930, forty-five-year-old Joseph Crater waved good-bye to friends after an evening meal in a New York restaurant, flagged down a taxi, and rode off. He was never seen or heard from again.

Fifty years of research has offered countless theories but no conclusions. Since Crater was a successful New York Supreme Court judge, many have suspected murder, but a solid lead has never been found. Other options have been presented: kidnapping, Mafia involvement, even suicide.

A search of his apartment revealed one clue. It was a note attached to a check, and both were left for his wife. The check was for a sizable amount, and the note simply read, "I am very weary. Love, Joe."

The note could have been nothing more than a thought at the end of a hard day. Or it could have meant a great deal more—the epitaph of a despairing man.

Weariness is tough. I don't mean the physical weariness that comes from mowing the lawn or the mental weariness that follows a hard day of decisions and thinking. No, the weariness that attacked Judge Crater is much worse. It's the weariness that comes just before you give up. That feeling of honest desperation. It's the dispirited father, the abandoned child, or the retiree with time on his hands. It's that stage in life when motivation disappears: the children grow up, a job is lost, a spouse dies. The result is weariness—deep, lonely, frustrated weariness.

Only one man in history has claimed to have an answer for it. He stands before all the Joseph Craters of the world with the same promise: "Come to me, all you who are weary . . . and I will give you rest" (Matthew 11:28).

Have you ever been truly weary? What do you do when you feel that way?

Have you ever known the rest Christ offers? If not, why not?

How do you place yourself in Christ's rest?

3
NOW, DON'T GET CARRIED AWAY!

Peter followed at a distance.
LUKE 22:54

Peter was sharp.

He kept his distance from Jesus.
"I'll stay close enough to see him," Peter reasoned.
"But not too close, or I may get caught."

Good thinking, Peter.

Don't get too involved—it might hurt.
Don't be too loyal—you might get branded.
Don't show too much concern—they'll crucify you, too.

We need more men like you, Peter.

Men who keep religion in its place.
Men who don't stir the water.
Men who reek with mediocrity.

That's the kind of man God needs, yessir.
>   *One who knows how to keep his distance:*
>   *"Now, I'll pay my dues and I'll come once a week,*
>   *but . . . well . . . you can get carried away, you know."*

Yes, you can get carried away . . .
>   *up a hill*
>   *to a cross*
>   *—and killed.*

Peter learned a lesson that day—a hard lesson.
>   *It is better to have never followed Jesus than to have*
>   *followed him and denied him.*

Mark these words:
>   *Follow at a distance and you'll deny the Master. Period.*
>   *You won't die for a man you can't touch. Period.*
>   *But stay near to him, in his shadow. . . .*
>   *You'll die with him, gladly.*

Have you been "carried away" by Jesus?

What keeps you at a distance? What do you need to give to God?

4
SOUR GRAPES

I once knew a man who treated Bible class and the worship service like a harsh movie critic treats a new release.

"Entertain me!"

Arms folded.

Lips tight.

Expectant.

"This had better be good."

With a ruthless eye and a critical ear
he sat
and watched
and listened.

The teacher, the minister, the music director—all were his prey. And woe be unto the teacher who didn't ask his opinion, unto the minister who went a few minutes over, unto the music director who chose songs the critic didn't know.

I once knew a man who came every Sunday to be entertained and not to encourage. He remarked that the Sunday afternoon game was more exciting than the Sunday morning assembly.

I wasn't surprised.

Sound familiar? What negative impact does this type of person have?

Have you ever felt like that man? What influences helped you shift your attitude?

5
BILLIE RESIGNS

One evening in 1954, Billie Sicard resigned from life. No official announcement was made, and no papers were signed. But still, she resigned. For all practical purposes, Billie decided to live no longer. Her spirit died in 1954; her body died in 1979.

On that evening in 1954, Billie's only reason to live left her. Her twelve-year-old son, George, died of a brain tumor. Little George's death left Billie prisoned inside a vacuum. She had been thirty-four when she had borne him. After her husband left, little George became her life. When he died, his death became hers.

She was well-to-do. Billie had lived on the exclusive Sunset Island in Miami since 1937. After her death the house went at an auctioned price of $226,000, a hefty sum for the time. Yet all this was immaterial to Billie. Her life had been her child.

They say that after George died in a New York City hospital, the body was brought to her home for a wake. After displaying the body for a day in the home of Mrs. Sicard, the funeral director came to remove it. She refused to let him. For several days she mourned behind locked doors before she gave the body up.

It was nothing for Billie to go on a shopping spree and spend a hundred dollars on toys for George. In 1979 when her body was found, so were the toys, exactly as her son had left them. Nothing was packed, nothing moved. For twenty-five years Billie had roamed in a house full of toys, with a heart full of memories. When the house was sold after her death, little George's Cub Scout uniform was still hanging in the down-stairs coat closet. On the wall was a child's sketch of a choo-choo train drawn in red crayon. She had never washed it off. His Mickey Mouse slippers sat in the corner of his bedroom. In the garage sat a 1941 Packard, a gift she had given to little George on his tenth birthday.

When Billie resigned from life, she became a social recluse. Her yard became a jungle. Her home became a source of ghost stories and old wives' tales. She overate. She withdrew. She didn't care.

Billie resigned.

Her life stands as a quiet legacy to us all. Man must have something larger than death . . . or death takes man.

Do you know someone who has "resigned" from life?

What keeps you engaged in life when difficulties strike?

How do you think God is calling you to live?

6

FOR THE LOVE
OF A STRANGER
AND THE LACK
OF A NAME

John's life peaked at age thirteen when he was homeroom president. So far, that office has been the high point in his life.

John's life is an enigma. Though he was born in a $300,000 home, he is known as a penniless drifter. Though he is the son of a successful oil tycoon, John quits more things than he finishes. Though his parents are gregarious and social, John is introverted, reclusive, almost stoic.

Friends suggest that he became a victim of his own failures. In a family of successes, he had made no name for himself. His brother and sister made it, but he didn't. The black sheep. The family failure. He had no name.

"Everything fits perfectly ... except John," one friend observed about the family.

College only added to the degeneration. He attended on

and off for seven years, never graduating. John was a loner at school, a lumpish young man with glassy eyes and a glower. One of the professors recalls, "There were usually empty chairs around him, as if he consciously chose to sit apart."

We don't know what emotions stirred within John. Anger, perhaps, at a society that only reminded him of his inadequacies. Guilt. Painful reminders that "I let everybody down." Nothingness. Barely known by those he touched, his passage was marked only by clutter and grime and confused scribbling.

We don't know the emotions, but we believe we know their result.

John Hinckley, Jr., seemed to have had every intention of killing the president. For the love of a stranger and the lack of a name, he allegedly emptied a revolver into the bodies of four men.

The latest report has John in a federal correctional facility in North Carolina. His room has a sink, toilet, single bed, one bulletproof window, and no TV or radio. He tried to overdose on Tylenol and failed. John can't kill a president, nor can he kill himself.

Our world has little room for failures. Our success-centered enterprise system is ideal for the successful but devastating for the loser. In an effort to create winners, we also create misfits.

Jesus had a place for misfits. In his book the last became first, and even the loser had value. It is our responsibility to be like Christ. It is our responsibility to intercept a life like John Hinckley's and fill it with value.

Where does our value come from?

Have you ever questioned your own value? Why?

How does a relationship with Christ affirm our value?

How can you put into action Christ's view of the misfits in your world?

7
MERCY, NOT
SACRIFICE

But go and learn what this means: "I desire mercy,
not sacrifice." For I have not come to call the
righteous, but sinners.

MATTHEW 9:13

"Lord," I said, "I want to be your man, not my own.
So to you I give my money, my car—even my home."

Then, smug and content, I relaxed with a smile
And whispered to God, "I bet it's been a while
Since anyone has given so much—so freely?"
His answer surprised me. He replied, "Not really.

"Not a day has gone by since the beginning of time,
That someone hasn't offered meager nickels and dimes,
Golden altars and crosses, contributions and penance,
Stone monuments and steeples; but why not repentance?

"The money, the statues, the cathedrals you've built,
Do you really think I need your offerings of guilt?
What good is money that's meant only to salve
The hurting conscience that so many of you have?

"Your lips know no prayers. Your eyes, no compassion.
But you will go to church (when churchgoing's in fashion).

"Just give me a tear—a heart ready to mold.
And I'll give you a mission, a message so bold—
That a fire will be stirred where there was only death,
And your heart will be flamed by my life and my breath."

I stuck my hands in my pockets and kicked at the dirt.
It's tough to be corrected (I guess my feelings were hurt).
But it was worth the struggle to realize the thought
That the Cross isn't for sale and Christ's blood can't be
bought.

What are you offering to Jesus? What gift does Jesus ask of you?

How do you truly embrace the sacrifice Jesus made?

8
WHO IS
RIGHTEOUS?

Question: O Lord, who shall live in your tent?

Answer: He who does what is right. (Psalm 15:1-2, paraphrased)

> *Have you ever noticed how many people want to be right*
> *before God?*
> *Rich people,*
> *Religious people,*
> *Nature people,*
> *City people.*

> *All kinds of people want to be right.*

> *Some people get educated:*
> *They learn all the funny little Greek symbols,*
> *they learn all about theology,*

they learn all about manuscripts, papyri, Dead Sea
    Scrolls,
and so on and on. . . .

They are righteous, they say . . . and they huddle together and
sneer at those who are not.

Some people get mission-minded:
    They learn new languages,
    they teach untaught people,
    they take pictures of converts and speak at conferences.

They are righteous, they say . . . and they all huddle together
and sneer at those who are not.

Some people get vocational:
    They get a job,
    they pay their own way,
    they rub elbows with the "real world,"
    they are drops of leaven in a swelling society.

They are righteous, they say . . . and they all huddle together
and sneer at those who are not.

You know, I think that sometimes God looks down at this
    dusty footstool and sees
    the righteous theological huddle,
    the righteous missionary huddle,
    the righteous vocational huddle

. . . and I think he sighs.

What is righteousness? Who is righteous?

Are you a "righteous huddler"? How can you break out of the huddle?

What is your attitude toward others? What should it be?

9

HOPE FOR LEO?

Let me introduce you to Leo.

I used to eat breakfast at a Cuban restaurant near my house. It was a brief, brisk walk and a good opportunity to think out my plans for the day. My thoughts were interrupted one morning, however, by a spry, unabashed old gent sporting a golf cap and dirty work pants. (He didn't look his sixty-six years.)

"You a student, son?" (I guess he saw my Bible and notebook.) "I've got some college textbooks for sale." I followed him into an empty house cluttered with lamps, books, end tables—all for sale. He was moving, he explained, "I need to get rid of this stuff." One topic led to another. Soon we were sitting and talking, Leo with his questions about the pope, the Bible, and "souls"; and me with my questions about Leo.

His history was colorful: "a depression kid"; sold franks at Yankee Stadium and programs at Madison Square Garden; a taxi driver in Miami. Yet although his life was full of experience, his face was void of joy. He spoke of how "You can't trust nobody no more. It's a hard world." When I tried to leave, he insisted that I stay. He was hungry for conversation. His fifth and last child had just left home. He said nothing about his marriage, though family portraits covered the wall. "I want to move . . . somewhere," he mumbled. Leo was in that era of life when all you have to look forward to is death and all you have to look back on is memories. To Leo, life was very real. To Leo, life was very empty.

Maybe it was unfair that I asked such a painful question, but I asked it anyway: "If you could live life all over again, would you?"

He looked at me and then at the floor. "No," he said sadly. "I don't think so."

It's hard to be without light in a dark world.

Do you ever feel that you are without that kind of light—even in your walk with Christ? Does life seem empty to you?

Do you experience the hope of Jesus?

How can you live in the peace and hope of Christ—and how can you share it with others?

10
JUDAS, THE MAN WHO NEVER KNEW

I've wondered at times what kind of man this Judas was. What he looked like, how he acted, who his friends were.

I guess I've stereotyped him. I've always pictured him as a wiry, beady-eyed, sly, wormy fellow, pointed beard and all. I've pictured him as estranged from the other apostles. Friendless. Distant. Undoubtedly he was a traitor and a quisling. Probably the result of a broken home. A juvenile delinquent in his youth.

Yet I wonder if that is so true. We have no evidence (save Judas's silence) that would suggest that he was isolated. At the Last Supper, when Jesus said that his betrayer sat at the table, we don't find the apostles immediately turning to Judas as the logical traitor.

No, I think we've got Judas pegged wrong. Perhaps he was just the opposite. Instead of sly and wiry, maybe he was robust and jovial. Rather than quiet and introverted, he could have been outgoing and well meaning. I don't know.

But for all the things we don't know about Judas, there is one thing we know for sure: He had no relationship with the Master. He had seen Jesus, but he did not know him. He had heard Jesus, but he did not understand him. He had a religion but no relationship.

As Satan worked his way around the table in the upper room, he needed a special kind of man to betray our Lord. He needed a man who had seen Jesus but who did not know him. He needed a man who knew the actions of Jesus but had missed out on the mission of Jesus. Judas was this man. He knew the empire but had never known the Man.

We learn this timeless lesson from the betrayer. Satan's best tools of destruction are not from outside the church; they are within the church. A church will never die from the immorality in Hollywood or the corruption in Washington. But it will die from corrosion within—from those who bear the name of Jesus but have never met him and from those who have religion but no relationship.

Judas bore the cloak of religion, but he never knew the heart of Christ. Let's make it our goal to know . . . deeply.

What qualities come to mind when you think of Judas? Do you share any of those characteristics?

What's the difference between having a religion and having a relationship?

11
THE HOPE THAT
WENT IGNORED

Once upon a time there was a tiny hamlet in the Swiss Alps. This hamlet was in serious trouble. The well that supplied water to the village went dry. The people began to panic. A river was near the community, but it was located at the bottom of a deep, deep gorge. Hence, no one could reach the water. And it was the middle of summer, so the snow on the mountain had long since melted.

There was, however, another well flowing with water across the gorge on the adjacent mountainside. An imaginative young thinker came up with a solution. He built a bridge across the gorge.

The villagers were elated.

A bucket brigade was formed immediately, and the water supply was replenished. Needless to say, the bridge became very important to this group. It was their source of life.

They honored the bridge. They named the bridge after the builder and painted it a beautiful gold. Tinsel was strung from the bridge. Miniature bridges were built and sold in the streets. People wore them on their necks and hung them in the windows. A committee was formed to pay homage to the bridge. Only certain people were allowed upon it, and then only on certain days, and then only when wearing certain clothes. The bridge keeper became the most respected and revered position on the mountain. No one could see or cross the bridge without his permission.

Unfortunately, there were disputes within the committee. The disagreement centered on whether a canopy should be built over the bridge. So the bridge was closed until a decision could be made.

Many villagers died of thirst while the leaders debated.

In the search for truth, the means often become the end.

What does this parable mean to you?

How was the villagers' thinking flawed?

What basic human characteristic caused the conflict? Have you seen this kind of faulty thinking in your world today?

12
EYES THAT NEVER SEE; EARS THAT NEVER HEAR

He's a deadly snake. Mark my words. Satan's snake. Be on your guard.

He's sly and wily. He lurks in every dark corner and musty hole. He strikes with abandon. The old, the rich, the poor, the young—all are his prey. He worms his way into every life and seldom misses his target.

And what slyness! We never know when he will strike. When he will creep up, we never know. All we see are the results of his deadly bite: blank faces, nonreflective hearts, questionless minds, empty lives. A trail cluttered with broken hearts and tears.

Who is this snake? Greed? Lust? Egotism? No (even though they are just as deadly). No, I'm unmasking the vilest of hell's vipers—complacence.

We live in a world plagued by complacence.

We're complacent to hope. Many people settle for a stale,

vanilla lifestyle that peaks at age seventeen. Hope? What's to hope for? Life is a paycheck and a weekend. Nothing more. You'd think we all had blinders. It's like one car after another driving off a cliff, no one daring to object. Like watercolor names painted on a sidewalk . . . washing away in an August rain.

We're complacent to death. Masked faces at a funeral endure the procession; weep at the burial; and then, a few hours later, giggle at the television comic. "The only way to handle death is to accept it as inevitable. Don't question it or defy it. You'll walk away depressed. Close your eyes. Put your hands over your ears. There is no explanation." We stand complacent.

We're complacent to God. Churchgoers pack the pews and sing to the back of someone's head. Fellowship is lost in formality. One, two, three times a week people pay their dues by walking in the door, enduring a ritual, and walking out. Guilt is appeased. God is insulted. Are we so naive as to think that he needs our attendance? Are we so ignorant that we put God in a box, thinking he can be taken in and out at our convenience?

We're complacent to purpose. How in the world can a person be born, be educated, fall in or out of love, have a job, be married, give birth, raise kids, see death, cry, scream, giggle, drink, eat, smoke, climb up or down the ladder, retire, and die without ever, ever asking why? Never asking "Why am I here?" Or, worse yet, asking why and being content with no answer. History is jam-packed with lives that died with no purpose. Neighborhoods reek with mediocrity. Office complexes are painted gray with boredom. Nine-to-fivers are hypnotized by routine. But does anyone object? Does anyone defy the machinery? Does anyone ask why?

Sometimes I want to stand at the corner of the street and yell, "Doesn't anyone want to know why? Why lonely evenings? Why broken hearts? Why abandoned marriages? Why fatherless babies?" But I never yell it. I just stick my hands in my pockets and stare . . . and wonder.

The most deadly trick of Satan is not to rob us of answers. It's to steal our questions.

What is the difference between contentment and complacency?

What is the source of complacency?

What would it take to shake your complacency?

13
NEW WINE IS FOR FRESH SKINS

I'll never forget Steven. I met him in St. Louis. His twenty-three years had been hard on him, his arm scarred from the needle and his wrist scarred from the knife. His pride was his fist, and his weakness was his girl.

Steve's initial response to love was beautiful. As we unfolded the story of Jesus before him, his hardened face would soften and his dark eyes would dance.

He wanted to change.

But his girlfriend would have none of it. Oh, she would listen politely and would be very sweet, but her heart was gripped by darkness. Any changes Steve made would be quickly muffled as she would craftily maneuver him back into his old habits. She was the last thing between him and the kingdom. We begged him to leave her. He was trying to put new wine into an old wineskin.

He wrestled for days trying to decide what to do. Finally, he reached a conclusion. He couldn't leave her.

The last time I saw Steve, he wept ... uncontrollably. I held big, tough, macho Steve in my arms. The prophecy of Jesus was true. By putting his new wine into an old skin, it was lost.

Think for a minute. Do you have any wineskins that need to be thrown out? Look closely in your closet. They come in all sizes. Maybe yours is an old indulgence—food, clothes, sex. Or an old habit, like gossip or profanity. Or possibly, like Steve, an old relationship. No friendship or romance is worth your soul. Repentance means change. And change means purging your heart of anything that can't coexist with Christ.

You can't put new life into an old lifestyle. The inevitable tragedy occurs. The new life is lost.

What are your old wineskins? What will it take for you to throw them out?

Are you willing to throw them out? If not—why not?

PART TWO

ON THE ANVIL

14
ON THE ANVIL

With a strong forearm, the apron-clad blacksmith puts his tongs into the fire, grasps the heated metal, and places it on the anvil. His keen eye examines the glowing piece. He sees what the tool is now and envisions what he wants it to be—sharper, flatter, wider, longer. With a clear picture in his mind, he begins to pound. His left hand still clutching the hot mass with the tongs, his right hand slams the two-pound sledge upon the moldable metal.

On the solid anvil, the smoldering iron is remolded.

The smith knows the type of instrument he wants. He knows the size. He knows the shape. He knows the strength.

Whang! Whang! The hammer slams. The shop rings with noise, the air fills with smoke, and the softened metal responds.

But the response doesn't come easily. It doesn't come without discomfort. To melt down the old and recast it as new is a disrupting process. Yet the metal remains on the anvil, allowing the toolmaker to remove the scars, repair the cracks, refill the voids, and purge the impurities.

And with time, a change occurs: What was dull becomes sharpened, what was crooked becomes straight, what was weak becomes strong, and what was useless becomes valuable.

Then the blacksmith stops. He ceases his pounding and sets down his hammer. With a strong left arm, he lifts the tongs until the freshly molded metal is at eye level. In the still silence, he examines the smoking tool. The incandescent implement is rotated and examined for any mars or cracks.

There are none.

Now the smith enters the final stage of his task. He plunges the smoldering instrument into a nearby bucket of water. With a hiss and a rush of steam, the metal immediately begins to harden. The heat surrenders to the onslaught of cool water, and the pliable, soft mineral becomes an unbending, useful tool.

"For a little while you may have had to suffer grief in all kinds of trials. These have come so that your faith—of greater worth than gold, which perishes even though refined by fire—may be proved genuine and may result in praise, glory and honor when Jesus Christ is revealed" (1 Peter 1:6-7).

Describe your own experiences with grief or difficult times. What have you learned through these experiences?

Has suffering affected your faith? In what ways?

15
ANVIL TIME

On God's anvil. Perhaps you've been there.

Melted down. Formless. Undone. Placed on the anvil for . . . reshaping? (A few rough edges too many.) Discipline? (A good father disciplines.) Testing? (But why so hard?)

I know. I've been on it. It's rough. It's a spiritual slump, a famine. The fire goes out. Although the fire may flame for a moment, it soon disappears. We drift downward. Downward into the foggy valley of question, the misty lowland of discouragement. Motivation wanes. Desire is distant. Responsibilities are depressing.

Passion? It slips out the door.

Enthusiasm? Are you kidding?

Anvil time.

It can be caused by a death, a breakup, going broke, going prayerless. The light switch is flipped off and the room darkens. "All the thoughtful words of help and hope have all been nicely said. But I'm still hurting, wondering. . . ."

On the anvil.

Brought face-to-face with God out of the utter realization that we have nowhere else to go. Jesus in the garden. Peter with a tear-streaked face. David after Bathsheba. Elijah and the "still, small voice." Paul, blind in Damascus.

Pound, pound, pound.

I hope you're not on the anvil. (Unless you need to be, and if so, I hope you are.) Anvil time is not to be avoided; it's to be experienced. Although the tunnel is dark, it does go through the mountain. Anvil time reminds us of who we are and who God is. We shouldn't try to escape it. To escape it could be to escape God.

God sees our life from beginning to end. He may lead us through a storm at age thirty so we can endure a hurricane at age sixty. An instrument is useful only if it's in the right shape. A dull ax or a bent screwdriver needs attention, and so do we. A good blacksmith keeps his tools in shape. So does God.

Should God place you on his anvil, be thankful. It means he thinks you're still worth reshaping.

Is it anvil time for you? What does that look like?

What is your hope for the reshaping that is taking place?

Has God left an imprint on your life? What does that mean to you?

16
FOOTPRINTS OF
SATAN

Once he was approached by a leper, who knelt before
him begging his help. "If only you will," said the man,
"you can cleanse me." In warm indignation Jesus
stretched out his hand, [and] touched him.

MARK 1:40-41, NEB

I was in an emergency room late one night last week.

Victims of Satan filled the halls.

A child—puffy, swollen eyes. Beaten by her father.

*A woman—bruised cheeks, bloody nose. "My boyfriend
got drunk and hit me," she said, weeping.*

*An old man—unconscious and drunk on a stretcher. He
drooled blood in his sleep.*

Jesus saw the victims of Satan, too.

*He saw a leper one day . . . fingers gnarled . . . skin
ulcerated . . . face disfigured.*

And he got indignant . . . angry.

Not a selfish, violent anger. A holy anger . . .

a controlled frustration . . .
a compassionate disgust.
And it moved him. It moved him to action.
I'm convinced that the same Satan stalks today,
    causing the hunger in Somalia . . .
    the confusion in the Mideast . . .
    the egotism on the movie screen . . .
    the apathy in Christ's church.
    And Satan giggles among the dying.
Dear Father,
    May we never grow so "holy," may we never be so
        "mature," may we never become so "religious," that
        we can see the footprints of Satan and stay calm.

What do you think is meant by "footprints of Satan"?

Does anything move you, as it does Jesus, to the kind of indignation described here?

Are you willing to stretch toward someone in need of your touch? Who might that be?

17

THUMP-THUD, THUMP-THUD

When a potter bakes a pot, he checks its solidity by pulling it out of the oven and thumping it. If it "sings," it's ready. If it "thuds," it's placed back in the oven.

The character of a person is also checked by thumping.

Been thumped lately?

Late-night phone calls. Grouchy teacher. Grumpy moms. Burnt meals. Flat tires. You've-got-to-be-kidding deadlines. Those are thumps. Thumps are those irritating inconveniences that trigger the worst in us. They catch us off guard. Flat-footed. They aren't big enough to be crises, but if you get enough of them, watch out! Traffic jams. Long lines. Empty mailboxes. Dirty clothes on the floor. Even as I write this, I'm being thumped. Because of interruptions, it has taken me almost two hours to write these two paragraphs. *Thump. Thump. Thump.*

How do I respond? Do I sing, or do I thud?

Jesus said that out of the nature of the heart a man speaks

(Luke 6:45). There's nothing like a good thump to reveal the nature of a heart. The true character of a person is seen not in momentary heroics but in the thump-packed humdrum of day-to-day living.

If you have a tendency to thud more than you sing, take heart.

There is hope for us "thudders":

1. Begin by thanking God for thumps. I don't mean a half-hearted thank-you. I mean a rejoicing, jumping-for-joy thank-you from the bottom of your heart (James 1:2). Chances are that God is doing the thumping. And he's doing it for your own good. So every thump is a reminder that God is molding you (Hebrews 12:5-8).
2. Learn from each thump. Face up to the fact that you are not "thump-proof." You are going to be tested from now on. You might as well learn from the thumps—you can't avoid them. Look upon each inconvenience as an opportunity to develop patience and persistence. Each thump will help you or hurt you, depending on how you use it.
3. Be aware of "thump-slump" times. Know your pressure periods. For me, Mondays are infamous for causing thump-slumps. Fridays can be just as bad. For all of us, there are times during the week when we can anticipate an unusual amount of thumping. The best way to handle thump-slump times? Head on. Bolster yourself with extra prayer, and don't give up.

Remember, no thump is disastrous. All thumps work for good if we are loving and obeying God.

Have you felt the divine Potter's thump lately? Why do you think he might be testing you?

If it's been a while since you've been thumped, why do you think that is?

Would you describe your spiritual attitude as singing, or thudding?

18
WHO PUSHES YOUR SWING?

Children love to swing. There's nothing like it. Thrusting your feet toward the sky, leaning so far back that everything looks upside down. Spinning trees, a stomach that jumps into your throat. Ahh, swinging. . . .

I learned a lot about trust on a swing. As a child, I only trusted certain people to push my swing. If I was being pushed by people I trusted (like Dad or Mom), they could do anything they wanted. They could twist me, turn me, stop me. . . . I loved it! I loved it because I trusted the person pushing me. But let a stranger push my swing (which often happened at family reunions and Fourth of July picnics), and it was *hang on, baby!* Who knew what this newcomer would do? When a stranger pushes your swing, you tense up, ball up, and hang on.

It's no fun when your swing is in the hands of someone you don't know.

Remember when Jesus stilled the storm in Matthew 8? The storm wasn't just a gentle spring rain. This was a *storm.*

Matthew calls the storm a *seismos,* which is the Greek word for "earthquake." The waves in this earthquake were so high that the boat was hidden. The Sea of Galilee can create a vicious storm. Barclay tells us that "on the west side of the water there are hills with valleys and gulleys; and when a cold wind comes from the west, these valleys and gulleys act like giant funnels. The wind becomes compressed in them and rushes down upon the lake with savage violence."

No sir, this was no spring shower. This was a storm deluxe. It was frightening enough to scare the pants (or robes) off of a dozen disciples. Even veteran fishermen like Peter knew this storm could be their last. So, with fear and water on their faces, they ran to wake up Jesus.

They ran to do what? Jesus was asleep? Waves tossing the boat like popcorn in a popper, and Jesus was asleep? Water flooding the deck and soaking the sailors, and Jesus was in dreamland? How in the world could he sleep through a storm?

Simple. He knew who was pushing the swing.

The disciples' knees were knocking because their swing was being pushed by a stranger. Not so with Jesus. He could find peace in the storm.

We live in a stormy world. At this writing wars rage in both hemispheres of our globe. World conflict is threatening all humanity. Jobs are getting scarce. Money continues to get tight. Families are coming apart at the seams.

Everywhere I look, private storms occur. Family deaths, strained marriages, broken hearts, lonely evenings. We must remember who is pushing the swing. We must put our trust in him. We can't grow fearful. He won't let us tumble out.

Who pushes your swing? In the right hands, you can find peace . . . even in the storm.

Are you swinging freely—or are you in the midst of a storm?

Do you find yourself learning to trust God more in either circumstance?

Do you really believe God is pushing your swing? Why?

19
JUAN—LUNCH

On Friday, May 7, my calendar reads *Juan—Lunch*. The lunch
date never occurred. Juan killed himself on Thursday, May 6.

Three weeks earlier Juan had spent a week in our house.
He'd just been dumped by a girl. Dumped hard. Several times
I saw him pull out a picture of them together, taken on New
Year's Eve. She was in an evening gown; Juan was in a tux.
"Boy, that was life in the big time," he'd say longingly, sadly.

He had tried twice before to kill himself but had failed.
This time he didn't fail. What makes a fellow do it? I really
wonder. What made him finally get the courage to do it? Juan
had breathed the exhaust of his own car.

Two days earlier I had run into him at Swenson's Ice
Cream Parlor.

He was there with some friends. We laughed some.

He seemed to be doing so well. (Where do we learn that
pain is something we have to hide?)

What emotions do I feel?

Confusion. The black veil of hopeless death falls viciously. Why? How horrid it is to be governed by laws we don't understand.

Guilt. You see, we were originally scheduled to have lunch on May 6, but I had postponed it to May 7. I can't help but wonder, *What if I hadn't canceled?* But the guilt will pass. I know too well my own failures. The inability to forgive oneself is itself suicidal.

Clarity. How death clears the fog! The abrupt departure of life starkly reminds me of why we are here. Death causes all other preoccupations of life to tumble down the hill, leaving at the top this one priority: Jesus Christ rose from the dead and God has forgiven my failures. When all we have to face is death and all we have to remember are memories, Jesus' victory and God's forgiveness will be the only things that matter.

Why am I writing this? It comforts me, for one thing. For another, I want you to know how terribly vital each person in the world is. I loved Juan. In a small way, this is a tribute to him. He was a victim of despair. He wanted a life he couldn't have. He had a life he couldn't handle.

Juan was caught in a shouting match between the world on one side and a handful of us on the other. "Life isn't worth it!" screamed the world. "Yes it is," we yelled back. "No it isn't." "Yes it is!" And there was Juan in the middle, caught and confused. He'd look at us—then at the world. A puppy between two masters. Finally, we were outshouted. "You're right, it isn't worth it!" He despaired and jumped.

But we can't quit shouting. Many may ignore us, but many will hear. And if only one hears, isn't it worth it?

Do you know someone whose words or actions betray a sense of despair? What could you do to extend an offer of hope?

Are you caught between two masters in any aspect of your life? What are they—and which master do you want to serve?

20
LIFE FROM THE
PRESS BOX

It made sense, after someone explained it to me, why our high
school football coach would always disappear in the middle
of the third quarter. I remember during my first game on the
varsity squad, I looked up from the sidelines (where I spent
most of my time) and noticed that he was gone. (It was a lot
quieter.) I couldn't figure out what had happened. I was afraid
the other team had kidnapped him. Or maybe he had gotten
sick on his chewing tobacco. So I asked a senior "sideliner."
(They know everything.)

"Where's the coach?" I asked, thinking I was the only
one to notice his absence, which made me feel important.

"In the press box," he answered.

"Getting coffee?" I asked.

"No, getting perspective."

Now that makes sense, doesn't it? There's no way a coach
can really keep up with the game from the sidelines. Everyone yelling advice. Parents complaining. Players screaming.

Cheerleaders cheering. Sometimes you've got to get away from the game to see it.

Occasionally we need to try that on ourselves, too. How vital it is that we keep a finger on the pulse of our own lives. How critical are those times of self-examination and evaluation. Yet it's hard to evaluate ourselves while we're in the middle of the game: schedules pressing, phones ringing, children crying.

I've got a suggestion. Take some press-box time. Take some time (at least half a day) and get away from everything and everyone.

Take your Bible and a notebook and get a press-box view of your life. Are you as in tune with God as you need to be? How is your relationship with your mate and children? What about your goals in life? Perhaps some decisions need to be made. Spend much time in prayer. Meditate on God's Word. Be quiet. Fast for the day.

Now, I'm not talking about a get-away-from-it-all day where you shop, play tennis, and relax in the sun (although such times are needed, too). I'm suggesting an intense, soul-searching day spent in reverence before God and in candid honesty with yourself. Write down your life story. Reread God's story. Recommit your heart to your Maker.

I might mention that a day like this won't just happen. It must be made. You'll never wake up and just happen to have a free day on your hands. (Those went out with your braces.) You'll have to pull out the calendar, elbow out a time in the schedule, and take it. Be stubborn with it. You need the time. Your family needs you to take this time.

Getting some press-box perspective could change the whole ball game.

What areas of your life require your focused attention or judgment?

In your quiet time with God, what truths has he revealed to you?

21

THE VALUE OF A
RELATIONSHIP

I used to visit George every Thursday when I lived in Miami. At the time I wasn't sure what kept drawing me to his musty little trailer. But looking back on it now, I think I know.

George had an unusual appearance: a patch over one eye ("I lost it in the war") and not a hair on his head. He was Canadian to the core and always kept the Maple Leaf draped in front of his trailer. Though over sixty, he swam and golfed daily and danced nightly. His voice boomed like a cannon when he talked, and he walked with such a pendulum swagger that he could have cleared a path for a bull.

But there was something much more profound about George that made me want to visit him. One summer day I realized what it was.

It was a hot Miami afternoon when I knocked on his door. He invited me in with his customary "Well hello, Max! Come on in here!" (He gave every visitor a glass of lemonade and some secret-recipe popcorn.) I stepped into the trailer.

"I've got someone I want you to meet," continued George with his Canadian twang. "My friend, Ralph."

I looked toward the corner. My eyes were still adjusting from the outside sun to the dimly lit trailer. As my vision cleared, I could see Ralph—and I wasn't sure what to think. There was a certain wildness about him: shoulder-length unkempt hair, a chest-length untamed beard. He was at least George's age, probably older. Apparently he didn't know what to think of me, either. His darting eyes sized me up from beneath his salt-and-pepper hair.

My palms began to sweat.

George interrupted the silence. "Sit down, Max. I've got something to show you." I sat on one side of the table while George scooted in next to Ralph across from me. "My most valued possession is right here."

I looked at his hands and then around the trailer.

"Where, George?"

"Right here." George put his big arm around Ralph's bony shoulders. "My most valued possession is my buddy. Ralph."

A new set of wrinkles appeared on Ralph's face as he broke into a toothless grin. Old friends. George and Ralph. Two crusty old travelers on the back curve of life's circle. They had found life's most precious element—a relationship.

Relationships. America's most precious resource. Take our oil, take our weapons, but don't take what holds us together— relationships. A nation's strength is measured by the premium it puts on its own people. When people value people, an impenetrable web is drawn, a web of vitality and security.

A relationship. The delicate fusion of two human beings. The intricate weaving of two lives; two sets of moods, mentalities, and temperaments. Two intermingling hearts, both seeking solace and security.

A relationship. It has more power than any nuclear bomb and more potential than any promising seed. Nothing will drive a man to greater courage than a relationship. Nothing will spawn greater devotion than a relationship. Nothing will fire the heart of a patriot or purge the cynicism of a rebel like a relationship.

Ah, but George said it best. "My most valued possession is my buddy."

What matters most in life is not what ladders we climb or what ownings we accumulate. What matters most is a relationship.

What steps are you taking to protect your "possessions"? What measure are you using to ensure that your relationships are strong and healthy? What are you doing to solidify the bridges between you and those in your world?

Do you resolve conflict as soon as possible, or do you "let the sun go down when you are still angry"? Do you verbalize your love every day to your mate and children? Do you look for chances to forgive? Do you pray daily for those in your life? Do you count the lives of your family members and friends more important than your own?

Our Master knew the value of a relationship. It was through relationships that he changed the world. His movement thrived not on personality or power but on championing the value of a person. He built bridges and crossed them.

Touching the leper . . . uniting the estranged . . . exalting the prostitute. And what was that he said about loving your neighbor as yourself?

It's a wise man who values people above possessions. Many wealthy men have died paupers because they gave their lives to things and not to people. And many paupers have left this earth in contentment because they loved their neighbors.

"My most valued possession is my buddy."

What is your most valued possession?

How would you describe your relationships?

Describe your most important relationship—the one with God.

22
NO MORE CURTAIN!

The annual event always drew a crowd. The priest would solemnly ascend the temple steps, bearing the blood of the sacrifice. As the people waited outside, he would pass through the great curtain and enter the Holy of Holies. He would sprinkle the mercy seat above the ark and pray that the blood would appease God. The sins would be rolled back. And the people would sigh with relief.

A great curtain hung as a reminder of the distance between God and man. It was like a deep chasm that no one could bridge. Man on his island . . . quarantined because of sin.

God could have left it like that. He could have left the people isolated. He could have washed his hands of the whole mess. He could have turned back, tossed in the towel, and started over on another planet. He could have, you know.

But he didn't.

God himself bridged the chasm. In the darkness of an eclipsed sun, he and a lamb stood in the Holy of Holies. He laid the lamb on the altar. Not the lamb of a priest or a Jew or a shepherd but the Lamb of God. The angels hushed as the blood of the Sufficient Sacrifice began to fall on the golden altar. Where had dropped the blood of lambs, now dripped the blood of life.

"Behold the Lamb of God."

And then it happened. God turned and looked one last time at the curtain.

"No more." And it was torn ... from top to bottom. Ripped in two.

"No more!"

"No more curtain!"

"No more sacrifices!"

"No more separation!"

And the sun came out.

Is there any way in which you are still living at a distance from God?

What is your attitude toward your sin? Do you think you have to appease God? Do you think you can?

Do you take the Lamb's sacrifice for granted?

23
HAVE YOU SEEN
JESUS?

One of the most dramatic scenes in the New Testament occurred in a city known as Caesarea Philippi. One would be hard-pressed to find a city with more elaborate religious significance than this one.

At least fourteen temples to Baal dotted the community. The Greeks heralded Caesarea Philippi as the home of the great god Pan, the god of nature. Jewish people pointed to the area around Caesarea Philippi as the source of the Jordan River; the significance of the Jordan River to the Jew was immeasurable. The might of Rome was glorified in a glistening marble temple erected in honor of Caesar. In Caesarea Philippi the Romans celebrated Caesar as divine and Rome as holy.

It must have been some city. Every significant nation and religion of the day was seen here: Syrians, Jews, Greeks, Romans. No modern metropolis can compare with Caesarea Philippi.

It was indeed a dramatic picture. In the midst of this carnival of marble columns and golden idols, a penniless, homeless, nameless Nazarene asks his band of followers, "Who do you say I am?" (Matthew 16:13-16).

The immensity of the question is staggering. I would imagine that Peter's answer did not come without some hesitation. Shuffling of feet. Anxious silence. How absurd that this man should be the Son of God. No trumpets. No purple robes. No armies. Yet there was that glint of determination in his eye and that edge of certainty in his message.

Peter's response sliced the silence. "I believe that you are . . . the Son of God."

Many have looked at Jesus, but few have seen him. Many have seen his shadow, his people, his story. But only a handful have seen Jesus. Only a few have looked through the fog of religiosity and found him. Only a few have dared to stand eye-to-eye and heart-to-heart with Jesus and say, "I believe that you are the Son of God."

What do you see when you consider Jesus of Nazareth? What do you believe about his claims?

What does your life say about what you believe?

If you haven't had an encounter with Jesus like this one lately, do you think you have given him a prominent place in your life?

24
A GOOD HEART,
BUT . . .

(Scene—Sunday a.m. assembly; silent prayer)

Max: God, I want to do great things.

God: You do?

Max: You bet! I want to teach millions! I want to fill the Rose Bowl! I want all of the world to know your saving power! I dream of the day—

God: That's great, Max. In fact, I can use you today after church.

Max: Super! How about some radio and TV work or . . . or . . . or an engagement to speak to Congress?

God: Well, that's not exactly what I had in mind. See that fellow sitting next to you?

Max: Yes.

God: He needs a ride home.

Max (quietly): What?

God: He needs a ride home. And while you're at it, one of the older ladies sitting near you is worried about getting a refrigerator moved. Why don't you drop by this afternoon and—

Max (pleading): But, God, what about the world?

God (smiling): Think about it.

Have you ever wanted to do something great for God?

Are you willing to obey him in small ways?

What opportunities for serving God are yours today?

25
THE HIKER

In the barren prairie, the hiker huddles down. The cold northerly sweeps over him, stinging his face and numbing his fingers. The whistle of the wind is deafening. The hiker hugs his knees to his chest, yearning for warmth.

He doesn't move. The sky is orange with dirt. His teeth are grainy, his eyes sooty. He thinks of quitting. Going home. Home to the mountains.

"Ahh. The mountains." The spirit that moved him in the mountains seems so far away. For a moment his mind wanders back to his homeland. Green country. Mountain trails. Fresh water. Hikers hiking on well-marked trails. No surprises, few fears, rich companionship.

One day, while on a brisk hike, he had stopped to look out from the mountains across the neighboring desert. He felt strangely pulled to the sweeping barrenness that lay before him. The next day he paused again. And the next, and the next. "Shouldn't someone go there? Shouldn't someone try to take life to the desert?" Slowly the flicker in his heart became a flame.

Many agreed that someone should go, but no one volunteered.

Uncharted land, fearful storms, loneliness.

But the hiker, spurred by the enthusiasm of others, determined to go. After careful preparation, he set out alone. With the cheers of his friends behind him, he descended the grassy highlands and entered the desolate wilderness.

The first few days his steps were springy and his eye was keen. He yearned to do his part to bring life to the desert. Then came the heat. The scorpions. The monotony. The snakes. Slowly, the fire diminished. And now . . . the storm. The endless roar of the wind. The relentless, cursed cold.

"I don't know how much more I can take." Weary and beaten, the hiker considers going back. "At least I got this far." Knees tucked under him, head bowed, almost touching the ground. "Will it ever stop?"

Grimly he laughs at the irony of the situation. "Some hiker. Too tired to go on, yet too ashamed to go home." Deep, deep is the struggle. No longer can he hear the voices of friends. Long gone is the romance of his mission. No longer does he float on the fancifulness of a dream.

"Maybe someone else should do this. I'm too young, too inexperienced." The winds of discouragement and fear whip at his fire, exhausting what is left of the flame. But the coals remain, hidden and hot.

The hiker, now almost the storm's victim, looks one last time for the fire. (Is there any greater challenge than that of stirring a spirit while in the clutches of defeat?) Yearning and clawing, the temptation to quit is gradually overcome by the urge to go on. Blowing on the coals, the hiker once again hears the call to the desert. Though faint, the call is clear.

With all the strength he can summon, the hiker rises to his feet, bows his head, and takes his first step into the wind.

Are you huddling down on the road you were called to walk?

When you're tempted to quit, do you question the call? Do you still hear it? Did it change?

Have you asked God to renew your sense of purpose lately? What is he asking you to do?

26
THE DAY MY PLATE
WAS BROKEN

It was past midnight in Dalton, Georgia, as I stood in a dimly lit phone booth making a call to my folks. My first summer job away from home wasn't panning out as it was supposed to. The work was hard. My two best friends had quit and gone back to Texas, and I was bunking in the Salvation Army until I could find an apartment.

For a big, tough nineteen-year-old, I sure felt small.

The voices of my mom and dad had never sounded so sweet. And although I tried to hide it, my loneliness was obvious. I had promised my parents that if they'd let me go, I'd stick it out for the whole summer. But now those three months looked like eternity.

As I explained my plight, I could tell my mom wanted me to come home. But just as she said, "Why don't you come—" my dad, who was on the extension, interrupted her. "We'd love for you to come back, but we've already broken your plate." (That was west Texas talk for "We love you, Max, but it's time to grow up.")

It takes a wise father to know when to push his son out of the nest. It's painful, but it has to be done. I'll always be thankful that my dad gave me wings and then made me use them.

What are some of the "nests" we get too comfortable in?

Have you ever had a positive plate-breaking experience like this one?

Do you need one now?

27
PUTTING YOUR BELIEFS WHERE YOUR HEART IS

Take a pen and paper and get alone. Go where it's quiet, where you can think. Find a place that will offer you an hour's worth of uninterrupted thinking. Then sit down. Take your pen in your hand and—are you ready?—write down what you believe. Not what you think or hope or speculate but what you *believe*. Put on paper those bedrock convictions that are worth building a life on, that are worth giving a life for.

For example, here are some not-for-sale, nonnegotiable undeniables that I believe:

There is a God whose all-consuming concern is whether or not I love him.

I have a reason to be alive.

Money is not the answer. Therefore, the abundance or lack of it will not rule me.

I will never die.

My family loves me and I love them.

I will live forever, and heaven is but a wink away.

I control my moods . . . not vice versa.

I can change my world.

The most important element in the world is another human being.

Now look at your list. Analyze it. What do you think? Is your foundation solid enough to stand on? If not, be patient. Give yourself some time to grow.

Don't throw that list away. Keep it. I've got a special assignment for you. Put your list someplace where you'll always have it. In your wallet, your purse . . . somewhere convenient.

The next time you're intimidated by Mr. Know-It-All or by Miss Have-It-All, the next time your self-image limps out the door, pull out your list. Take a long look at it. Have any of your undeniables been threatened? Has your foundation been attacked?

Usually not. Here's the point: If you know what you believe (I mean *really* know it), if you know what's important and what's trivial, then you won't be tied down by all the little Lilliputians in the world.

I *really* believe that.

28
SOMEDAY

Thousands of years before Jesus was called the Lamb of God, God promised forgiveness.

"Someday," he promised Hosea. "Someday, I will remember their sins no more."

"Someday," God confided to Jeremiah, "these people will be my people and I will be their God."

"And someday," wrote David, "the mistakes of men will be tossed, not under a rug or behind the sofa, but far, far away. As far as the east is from the west."

And do you know what? That someday came. On a garbage heap outside of Jerusalem.

Someday the almighty God, who has every right to make me burn forever, will look past my apathy, my gluttony, my lying, and my lusting. He will point to the cross and invite me to come home . . . forgiven . . . forever.

How do you view your sins? As if they can be swept under the rug, or as permanent blots on your record?

Look at the promises of God shown in this chapter. What do you believe they say about you and your sins?

For those of us who already know forgiveness of sins now, through Jesus, what is the significance of "someday"?

29
"GOD, DON'T YOU CARE?"

Teacher, don't you care if we drown?
MARK 4:38

Such an honest cry, a doggedly painful cry. I've asked that one before, haven't you? It's been screamed countless times. . . .

A mother weeps over a stillborn child. A husband is torn from his wife by a tragic accident. The tears of an eight-year-old fall on a daddy's casket. And the question wails.

"God, don't you care?" "Why *me?*" "Why *my* friend?" "Why *my* business?"

It's the timeless question. The question asked by literally every person that has stalked this globe. There has never been a president, a worker, or a businessman who hasn't asked it. There has never been a soul who hasn't wrestled with this aching question. Does my God care? Or is my pain God's great goof?

As the winds howled and the sea raged, the impatient and frightened disciples screamed their fear at the sleeping Jesus.

"Teacher, don't you care that we are about to die?" He could have kept on sleeping. He could have told them to shut up. He could have impatiently jumped up and angrily dismissed the storm. He could have pointed out their immaturity. . . . But he didn't.

With all the patience that only one who cares can have, he answered the question. He hushed the storm so the shivering disciples wouldn't miss his response. Jesus answered once and for all the aching dilemma of man: Where is God when I hurt?

Listening and healing. That's where he is. He cares.

Have you ever been in a life storm and thought God was asleep, or at least looking somewhere else? Are you in one now?

When God silences your storm, how do you respond?

30
THE BLUNTED AX

Until the Cross, Satan held a cruel ax over man's head. All feared the ax of death. Its eerie glimmer humbled all who faced it. From the greatest to the smallest, all avoided the ax. Satan's mysterious, abrupt blade severed man from the living and cast him into the unknown.

For centuries men had appeased the ax, evaded the ax, ignored the ax. But its razor-sharp edge made victims of all, relentlessly marching each to the chopping block, sweeping down upon mankind an execution that none could escape.

Until the Cross. It was at the Cross that the power of the ax was dissolved and its true weakness disclosed. With all of the strength that Satan could muster and all the cruelty he could display, he brought the ax down upon the neck of the Son of God. The savage blow rang throughout the forest of death and echoed across the universe.

"I have done it!" Satan laughed. His wiry figure contorted with laughter. "I have killed life." The triumphant scream echoed in the chambers of Hades. And for a brief, fearful moment, all humanity gasped.

But the Divine Figure was not to be trapped. His body rose from the block, his head still intact, his life surviving. Jesus had blunted the ax. Jesus had flouted the executioner's threat. Turning to Satan, he posed the question that paved the path to immortality. "Where, O death, is your victory? Where, O death, is your sting?"

What is this "ax of death"? What does it mean for us today?

Does death still have a sting for us—for you? How?

How does the Cross dissolve the power of death?

31

VALENTINE'S DAY, 1965

My decision had been made sometime during the week. I didn't tell a soul. (For a ten-year-old, I kept a good secret.) I think I reached my decision on a Monday . . . or maybe Tuesday. Nonetheless, after the decision was made, Sunday took forever to arrive.

But Sunday finally came. *The* Sunday. *My* Sunday.

Mom didn't have to wake me that day. I was up before her. It just so happened that it was Valentine's Day. I hardly noticed. I remember polishing my "church shoes" until I could see my face in the reflection. An extra palmful of Vitalis was needed on my short red hair to keep my rooster tail from popping up. My daddy tied my tie for me. I washed my face so hard my freckles almost came off.

I was nervous during Sunday school, glad when it was over. Butterflies were swarming in my stomach. The assembly, however, seemed to settle my nervous energy. I sang louder than ever and hung on every word of the sermon. The butterflies stopped. I don't remember questioning the decision. It seemed so obvious, so right.

The invitation song had hardly begun when I made my move. The five or six steps I had to make, I made fast. So fast that no one saw me go forward except those near the front.

I told our preacher I wanted to be baptized into Jesus. With an innocent faith that children so easily have, I asked God to take over. Did I understand all the implications of my conversion? No. All I knew was that Jesus' love awaited those who would respond to it, so I did. Ever since that day the Creator of the world—the almighty God—has watched over me like a daddy over a baby, loving me as I have never deserved and sticking with me when others left.

It was the most beautiful day of my life. What a wonderful Valentine's Day!

What is your "Valentine's" story with God? Is it a story that you cherish?

How have you asked God to take over your life? Take some time to reflect on your decision and how your life has changed since then.

32
OPEN MANHOLES
AND SUDDEN SIN

It happens in an instant. One minute you are walking and whistling, the next you are wide-eyed and falling. Satan yanks back the manhole cover, and an innocent afternoon stroll becomes a horror story. Helplessly you tumble, aware of the fall but unable to gain control. You crash at the bottom and stare blankly into the darkness. You inhale the evil stench and sit in Satan's sewage until he spits you out and you land, dumbfounded and shell-shocked, on the sidewalk.

Such is the pattern of sudden sin. Can you relate to it? Very few sins are premeditated and planned. Very few of us would qualify for Satan's strategy team. We spend our time avoiding sin, not planning it. But don't think for one minute that, just because you don't want to fall, you won't. Satan has a special trick for you, and he only pulls it out when you aren't looking.

This yellow-bellied father of lies doesn't dare meet you face-to-face. No sir. Don't expect this demon of demons to challenge you to a duel. Not this snake. He hasn't the integrity to tell you to turn around and put up your dukes. He fights dirty.

He is the master of the trapdoor and the author of weak moments. He waits until your back is turned. He waits until your defense is down. He waits until the bell has rung and you are walking back to your corner. Then he aims his dart at your weakest point and . . .

Bull's-eye! You lose your temper. You lust. You fall. You take a drag. You buy a drink. You kiss the woman. You follow the crowd. You rationalize. You say yes. You sign your name. You forget who you are. You walk into her room. You look in the window. You break your promise. You buy the magazine. You lie. You covet. You stomp your feet and demand your way.

You deny your Master.

It's David disrobing Bathsheba. It's Adam accepting the fruit from Eve. It's Abraham lying about Sarah. It's Peter denying that he ever knew Jesus. It's Noah, drunk and naked in his tent. It's Lot, in bed with his own daughters. It's your worst nightmare. It's sudden. It's sin.

Satan numbs our awareness and short-circuits our self-control. We know what we are doing and yet can't believe that we are doing it. In the fog of weakness, we want to stop but haven't the will to do so. We want to turn around but our feet won't move. We want to run, and pitifully, we want to stay.

It's the teenager in the backseat. It's the alcoholic buying "just one." It's the boss touching his secretary's hand. The husband walking into the porn shop. The mother losing her temper. The father beating his child. The gambler losing his money. The Christian losing control. And it's Satan gaining a foothold.

Confusion. Guilt. Rationalization. Despair. It all hits. It hits hard. We numbly pick ourselves up and stagger back into our world. "O God, what have I done?" "Should I tell someone?" "I'll never do it again." "My God, can you forgive me?"

No one who is reading these words is free from the treachery of sudden sin. No one is immune to this trick of perdition. This demon of hell can scale the highest monastery wall, penetrate the deepest faith, and desecrate the purest home.

Some of you know exactly what I mean. You could write these words better than I, couldn't you? Some of you, like me, have tumbled so often that the stench of Satan's breath is far from a novelty. You've asked for God's forgiveness so often that you worry that the well of mercy might run dry.

Want to sharpen your defenses a bit? Do you need help in reinforcing your weaponry? Have you tumbled down the manhole one too many times? Then consider these ideas:

First, *recognize Satan*. Our war is not with flesh and blood but with Satan himself. Do like Jesus did when Satan met him in the wilderness. Call him by name. Rip off his mask. Denounce his disguise. He appears in the most innocent of clothing: a night out with the boys, a good book, a popular movie, a pretty neighbor. But don't let him fool you! When the urge to sin rears its ugly head, look him squarely in the eye and call his bluff. "Get behind me, Satan!" "Not this time, you dog of hell! I've walked your stinking corridors before. Go back to the pit where you belong!" Whatever you do, don't flirt with this fallen angel. He'll thresh you like wheat.

Second, *accept God's forgiveness.* Romans chapter 7 is the Emancipation Proclamation for those of us who have a tendency to tumble. Look at verse 15: "I do not understand what I do. For what I want to do I do not do, but what I hate I do."

Sound familiar? Read on. Verses 18 and 19: "For I have the desire to do what is good, but I cannot carry it out. For what I do is not the good I want to do; no, the evil I do not want to do—this I keep on doing."

Man, that fellow has been reading my diary!

"What a wretched man I am! Who will rescue me from this body of death?" (verse 24).

Please, Paul, don't stop there! Is there no oasis in this barrenness of guilt? There is. Thank God and drink deeply as you read verse 25 and verse 1 of chapter 8: "Thanks be to God—through Jesus Christ our Lord! . . . Therefore, there is now no condemnation for those who are in Christ Jesus."

Amen. There it is. You read it right. Underline it if you wish. For those *in* Christ there is *no* condemnation. Absolutely none. Claim the promise. Memorize the words. Accept the cleansing. Throw out the guilt. Praise the Lord. And . . . watch out for open manholes.

Think about the idea of Satan's "special tricks." Which ones tend to work on you?

What steps do you need to take to keep yourself from the manholes of those "sudden sins"?

What hope is there for us who are so susceptible to sin?

33
WHO'S IN CHARGE HERE?

Ever have trouble determining God's will for your future? You're not alone. "Do I move to Mobile, or Minnesota?" "Do I retire, or keep working?" "An engineer at IBM, or a clerk at Sears?" "Do I marry, or stay single?" The questions are endless. One follows another. Every new responsibility brings new decisions. "What college should my son attend?" "Is it time for children?" "Should I live near the church, or commute?"

How in the world do we know what God wants? Do we set out a fleece? seek advice? pray? read the Bible? All these are right, yet there is one decision that must be made first. (Hang on, it's a tough one.)

To know God's will, we must totally surrender to God's will. Our tendency is to make God's decision for him. I used to do that with my mom. As a child, I hated to get the flu for two reasons: (1) it hurt, and (2) my mom was a nurse. Since she was an RN, she knew the fastest way to tackle the flu bug was with a needle . . . in my bottom. Ouch! (I grew up thinking penicillin was a dirty word.)

When she would tell me to "go get the medicine," I would get everything but the dreaded needle. I'd come back with an armful: aspirin, Pepto-Bismol, ear drops, nose drops, ankle wraps—anything but penicillin. But, as good moms do, she always got her point across. "Now, you know better," she'd say with a smile, and I would go to get the (gulp) needle.

Here's the point. Don't go to God with options and expect him to choose one of your preferences. Go to him with empty hands—no hidden agendas, no crossed fingers, nothing behind your back. Go to him with a willingness to do whatever he says. If you surrender your will, then he will "equip you with everything good for doing his will" (Hebrews 13:21).

It's a promise.

What decisions do you face today: big ones, small ones?

Have you ever seen God guide you toward a particular choice? How do you usually ask for his help?

How full of options are your hands? Could you empty them before the Lord and accept his will—before you sense his direction?

PART THREE

AN INSTRUMENT FOR NOBLE PURPOSES

34
AN INSTRUMENT
FOR NOBLE
PURPOSES

... made holy, useful to the Master and prepared
to do any good work.
2 TIMOTHY 2:21

Ah, to be your instrument, O God,
like Paul to the Gentiles,
like Philip to the eunuch,
like Jesus to the world,
... to be your instrument.
To be like a scalpel in the gentle hands of a surgeon,
healing and mending.
To be like a plow in the weathered hands of a farmer,
sowing and tending.
To be like a scythe in the sweeping hands of a reaper,
gathering and using.
To be ... an instrument for noble purposes.
To be honed and tuned,

in sync with your will,
sensitive to your touch.
This, my God, is my prayer.
Draw me from your fire,
form me on your anvil,
shape me with your hands,
and let me be your tool.

Where is your heart today? Do you desire to be used of God?

What might it take for you to be shaped by God's hands, in sync with his will?

Think of those images of God: as surgeon, farmer, reaper. Is the Lord showing you a way to use your gifts to help others?

35
TODAY I WILL MAKE A DIFFERENCE

Today I will make a difference. I will begin by controlling my thoughts. A person is the product of his thoughts. I want to be happy and hopeful. Therefore, I will have thoughts that are happy and hopeful. I refuse to be victimized by my circumstances. I will not let petty inconveniences such as stoplights, long lines, and traffic jams be my masters. I will avoid negativism and gossip. Optimism will be my companion, and victory will be my hallmark. Today I will make a difference.

I will be grateful for the twenty-four hours that are before me. Time is a precious commodity. I refuse to allow what little time I have to be contaminated by self-pity, anxiety, or boredom. I will face this day with the joy of a child and the courage of a giant. I will drink each minute as though it is my last. When tomorrow comes, today will be gone forever. While it is here, I will use it for loving and giving. Today I will make a difference.

I will not let past failures haunt me. Even though my life is scarred with mistakes, I refuse to rummage through my trash heap of failures. I will admit them.

I will correct them. I will press on. Victoriously. No failure is fatal. It's okay to stumble. . . . I will get up. It's okay to fail. . . . I will rise again. Today I will make a difference.

I will spend time with those I love. My spouse, my children, my family. A man can own the world but be poor for the lack of love. A man can own nothing and yet be wealthy in relationships. Today I will spend at least five minutes with the significant people in my world. Five *quality* minutes of talking or hugging or thanking or listening. Five undiluted minutes with my mate, children, and friends.

Today I will make a difference.

Are you letting petty inconveniences—or not-so-petty circumstances—master you? Or is God your master in all things?

What are you grateful for?

What difference would you like to make in this one day you're given?

36
THE TESTED
TUNNEL

We held our breath as he disappeared into the tunnel. There were five of us. Five energetic boys. School was out for the summer, so we had turned our attention to the vacant lot next to our house. The flat, west Texas land was a perfect summer playground.

On this particular day, it seemed that the attention of the entire world was focused on that tunnel. We had dug a ditch about three feet wide and four feet deep that ran half-way across the lot. To give it the appearance of a tunnel, we covered it with several planks of scavenged plywood and a thick layer of dirt. We camouflaged the entrance and exit with a few tumbleweeds and mesquite bushes, and—presto!—we had an underground tunnel. It was ready to entertain an entire neighborhood of ruffians as they fought off Indians, escaped from slavery, and invaded Normandy.

Today was the day we would test the tunnel. Was it strong enough? wide enough? deep enough? too long? Would it collapse? The only way to find out was to send a volunteer through the tunnel first. (Memory may fail me here, but I think it was my brother who agreed to test the tunnel.)

It was a tense moment. The five of us stood solemnly in our T-shirts and jeans. We gave him last words of encouragement. We patted him on the back. (We admired his self-sacrifice.) We stood quietly as he decisively got down on hands and knees and scurried into the hole. We held our breath as we watched the soles of his high-top sneakers disappear into the darkness.

No one spoke as we waited. The only movement was the pounding of our young hearts. Our eyes stayed fixed on the tunnel exit.

Finally, after we had each died a thousand deaths, my brother's sandy blond hair emerged from the other end. I can remember his triumphant fist leading the way as he scrambled out, yelling, "There's nothing to it! Don't worry!" And who could argue with the testimony of seeing him alive and well, jumping up and down at the tunnel's exit? We all went in!

There is something about a living testimony that gives us courage. Once we see someone else emerging from life's dark tunnels, we realize that we, too, can overcome.

Could this be why Jesus is called our pioneer? Is this one of the reasons that he consented to enter the horrid chambers of death? It must be. His words, though persuasive, were not enough. His promises, though true, didn't quite allay the fear of the people. His actions, even the act of calling Lazarus from the tomb, didn't convince the crowds that death was nothing to fear. No. In the eyes of humanity, death was still the black veil that separated them from joy. There was no victory over this hooded foe. Its putrid odor invaded the nostril of every human, convincing them that life was only meant to end abruptly and senselessly.

It was left to the Son of God to disclose the true nature of this force. It was on the cross that the showdown occurred. Christ called for Satan's cards. Weary of seeing humanity fooled by a cover-up, he entered the tunnel of death to prove that there was indeed an exit. And as the world darkened, creation held her breath.

Satan threw his best punch, but it wasn't enough. Even the chambers of Hades couldn't stop this raider. Legions of screaming demons held nothing over the Lion of Judah.

Christ emerged from death's tunnel, lifted a triumphant fist toward the sky, and freed all from the fear of death.

"Death has been swallowed up in victory!"

Do you fear the tunnel of death? Or, how is death swallowed up in victory in your life?

What other dark tunnels do you face? Can you take courage from the testimony of others who have faced similar circumstances?

What about your own testimony? Have you been given, through trial, an ability to cheer on someone else? Are you doing that?

37
THE MOVEMENT
THAT WAS
DOOMED TO FAIL

From the start the movement was doomed to fail. For one thing it began with just 120 men. Remarkably few, when you consider that their homeland had a population of four million. Besides that, most of the men were illiterate and poor. Blue-collar workers they were, far too ignorant to stage an uprising that could make any difference.

Few, if any, had traveled beyond their own country. They were inexperienced and uncultured. Their nation was oppressed. Their people were weary. Their government was corrupt. Their religion was shallow.

The strategy of the movement was disastrous. No head-quarters was ever established. No professional research was ever done. Plans were made by the seat of the pants. The leaders couldn't even agree on the exact definition of their mission.

On top of all of this, the movement was impractical. It was far too extreme and absurd. It demanded too much too soon. It lacked any tact. It was too impatient with traditions. It called for a reversal of social classes. It gave too much leverage to women and minority groups.

The movement was doomed to failure.

But it didn't fail. It succeeded. Not only did it succeed but it far surpassed any movement in our world's history. Within thirty years the message of Jesus Christ had entered every port, city, and courtyard of the world. It was infectious. It was a moving organism. People actually died to see it continue.

It should have failed, but it succeeded. And it still succeeds. God's movement will never stop. Some say that the United States is a post-Christian nation. That doesn't matter. Others scoff at the absurdity of believing in anything absolute. That won't stop it. Materialism blankets the country. Still the movement will continue. It might be slowed, but it will never be stopped.

The church might bicker and fight. The people might grow crusty with traditions. The leaders may grow nearsighted. But the movement will march on. Nothing will ever stop it. The Judean Commander can't be stilled.

We should fall to our knees in humble gratitude that God has allowed us to participate in such a cause. For this is not the movement of a man. It is the movement of God. That is precisely why what should have failed will never fail. It is the movement of God.

What is this "movement" of God? What do you know about the mission of Jesus Christ on this earth?

What would you say is the central message, the core belief that has held together and defined the Christian movement all these years?

How do you fit in to the movement? Are you an advancer of the cause?

38
COMMUNICATION
IS MORE THAN
WORDS

There are basically two types of people who engage in conversations: those who want to communicate and those trying to show off. The latter is usually a self-styled expert on everything. He can't resist the temptation to toss his opinion in the ring. He is the fellow who makes a comment in class in order to be noticed by others rather than to learn from others.

The true expert on a topic never needs to put others down in order to elevate himself. Nor does he need to employ foreign technical jargon in communicating with the lay public. Such jargon is useful among professionals but is basically useless elsewhere.

In religion we have developed our own jargon—words like *salvation, sanctification, holiness,* and *reconciliation*. These are words that are invaluable and significant to us, but they do not always communicate to the non-Christian.

One of the paradoxes of communication is that a word

must be understandable to both parties before it is acceptable for use. Just because *you* understand a word or concept doesn't mean that the person with whom you are speaking does. The communicator, then, is responsible to select words that are acceptable to both parties. To use long and lanky words just because they are long and lanky may be impressive, but it's certainly not good communication. To throw words in the air and assume that they will be understood is irresponsible and selfish.

E. H. Hutten tells a beautiful story about Albert Einstein. It's a good example of how the expert who knows his "stuff" has no need or desire to impress others. While at Princeton, Einstein would occasionally attend lectures by scientists who often were somewhat obscure and technical in their expression and presentation. As Hutten relates it,

> Einstein would rise after the lecture and ask whether he might put a question. He would then go to the blackboard and begin to explain in simple terms what the lecturer had been talking about. "I wasn't quite sure I understood you correctly," he would say with great gentleness, and then would make clear what the lecturer had been unable to convey.

This is what effective communication is all about. Jesus was a master at never assuming that something was communicated just because it was spoken. He employed endless creativity: illustrations, parables, quizzes, questions, case studies, and so on. Aquinas said long ago, "The poor teacher stands where he is and beckons the pupil come to him. The good teacher goes to where the pupil is, takes him, and leads him to where he ought to go."

Is it more important to you to be right—or to communicate?

As a Christian, what do you hope to communicate to those in your world?

How do you approach the Great Commission of Jesus: Are you waiting for the pupil to come to you? Is there someone to whom you ought to go?

39
NONNEGOTIABLE LOVE

It was a long summer. I was thirteen, a left fielder on the local Pony League team. I held the record for the most strikeouts . . . as a batter, not as a pitcher. I went the entire season and got only two hits. Over sixty times at bat and only two hits.

Two hits! That's not even good enough to be called a slump! That's a lot of long walks from the plate to the dugout. It got to the point where my team moaned when my time at bat was called. (The other team cheered.) Pretty tough on the self-image of a thirteen-year-old who had dreams of playing for the Dodgers.

The only thing right that summer was my parents' attitude toward my "slump." They never missed a game. Never. Not once did I look up and see their bleacher seats unoccupied. I was still their boy even if I led the league in strikeouts. Their commitment ran deeper than my performance. They showed me the importance of an unwavering commitment.

The Old Testament contains the beautiful story of Naomi

and Ruth, a mother-in-law and daughter-in-law who both lost their husbands. Naomi, a foreigner in Ruth's homeland, yearns to return to her own country. Ruth, still young and marriageable, displays her loyalty to her mother-in-law by going with her and providing for her well-being. The determination and commitment of Ruth are evident in her words: "Where you go I will go, and where you stay I will stay. Your people will be my people and your God my God. Where you die I will die, and there I will be buried" (Ruth 1:16-17).

One relationship of this caliber can buoy us through the fiercest storms. It was the Beatles who sang, "Will you still need me, will you still feed me, when I'm sixty-four?" Oh, the agony of being sixty-four (or any age, for that matter) and having no one to care for you or need you. Happy are those who have one companion, one relationship that is not based on looks or performance. Every person is in dire need of at least one faithful friend or a mate who will look them in the eye and say, "I will never leave you. You may grow old and gray, but I'll never leave you. Your face may wrinkle and your body may ruin, but I'll never leave you. The years may be cruel and the times may be hard, but I'll be here. I will never leave you."

Think for a minute about the people in your world. What do they think of your commitment to them? How would you rate your faithfulness? Does your loyalty ever waver? Do you have one person with whom your "contract" is nonnegotiable?

Once, two friends were fighting together in a war. The combat was ferocious, and many lives were being taken. When one of the two young soldiers was injured and could not get back to the trenches, the other went out to get him against his officer's orders. He returned mortally wounded, and his friend, whom he had carried back, was dead.

The officer looked at the dying soldier, shook his head, and said, "It wasn't worth it."

The young boy, overhearing the remark, smiled and said, "But it *was* worth it, sir, because when I got to him he said, 'Jim, I knew you'd come.'"

Make the most of your relationships. Follow the advice of Benjamin Franklin: "Be slow in choosing friends and be even slower in leaving them."

Why is it important for us to be faithful in our various relationships? What model do we have?

Are you a faithful friend? spouse? family member?

40
SINGLEHOOD: MISTAKE OR MISSION?

In our culture we have certain things that we simply don't know how to handle: nuclear reactors, inflation, pornography, and perhaps the most confusing of all, single people.

Single people. What an enigma! Those unusual creatures without wives or husbands. What do you say to them? How can you carry on a conversation with people who are so deprived and socially amputated? Do you pity them? encourage them? ignore them? Our culture is built so much around the home that those without a home are . . . well, they're kind of like a plane without a hangar (high-flying, but nowhere to go in a storm).

Once, before I was married, I took a trip to visit my old alma mater. I saw a lot of old friends. Married friends, professors, ex-classmates, ministers, old girlfriends. Their response to my still-matelessness was amusing.

"Haven't found the right one yet?" they'd inquire. "Gee, Max, I'm sorry." (As though I'd failed at life.)

Some were more tactful. "How's your social life?" (What they really wanted was a scouting report.)

"Fine," I'd say. (I got a kick out of leaving them wondering.)

"Oh." They'd get nervous and then close in with something more discreet: "What about Saturday nights?" Wink.

Others had pity on me. Several put their arms around my shoulders or gently took my hand (as though I were terminally ill) and confided, "God has one waiting for you, Max. Don't be afraid." (Was it my imagination or did I detect a little sympathetic rubbing on the ringless finger?)

I know people mean well. But, honestly . . . is bachelorhood really a disease? Are life and meaning found only at the marriage altar? Is there no room at the inn for those who sleep alone? Are they that socially underdeveloped?

Jesus suggested that singleness is more than acceptable. In fact, Jesus called it a gift (Matthew 19:12); not for everybody but for a few. A gift that encourages "undivided devotion to the Lord" (1 Corinthians 7:35). Perhaps, then, a single Christian should not be regarded as one who is spiritually impotent but as one who is gifted. I was grateful for my "gift" of singleness. Later God chose to replace my gift with a wife. I'm thankful, and I'm still serving him. But, believe it or not, it is possible to be content and come home to an empty apartment.

Being mateless is not nearly as bad as it's made out to be. In fact, it could be part of a plan.

How do you view the singles in your world?

How can you model Jesus' attitude toward singles in your encounters with those who are unmarried?

41
THE POISON
TONGUE

I once knew an extremely courageous lady. She was courageous for several reasons. For one thing, she was waging an
uphill battle against alcoholism. For another, she was doing all
she could to restore her relationship with God. It's tough to
start over. It's even tougher to start over when people won't
let you.

She chose a small church to attend, a church where she
knew many members. She thought she'd be received there.
One Sunday she parked her car near the church building and
got out. As she walked toward the front door, she overheard
two ladies talking nearby. The stinging words were not meant
for her ears, but she heard them anyway.

"How long is that alcoholic going to hang around
here?"

She turned and went back to the car. She never entered
another church building until she died. Those ladies meant no
harm, yet seemingly painless gossip did irreparable damage.

These five ideas will help us control our tongues:

1. Never say anything about someone that you wouldn't say to his face.
2. Never say anything about someone unless she is there to respond.
3. Refuse to listen to someone else's gossip.
4. Initiate positive statements about people whom you're discussing.
5. Remember, "the tongue . . . is a fire" (James 3:6).

Do you listen to—or contribute to—gossip?

Is it your habit to think and speak well of others?

Does your tongue need taming? What does the Lord desire of you—and how will you seek to obey him?

42
THE DAY OF THE
QUESTION. THE
QUESTION!

The day began simply enough. Saturday morning. I slept an
hour later than usual. The morning sun greeted my slow-
opening eyes. In groggy semiconsciousness I rolled over,
enjoying the slower weekend pace. "Heaven will be an eternal
Saturday morning. . . ." Fantasy.

Then I remembered. My eyes popped open. "Today is
the day." I swallowed hard. The day of the question. *The* question. It turned out to be quite a day. In fact, I've never had a
day quite like it.

Twilight zone. Dream world. Did I shower? I don't
remember. We had breakfast. Went shopping. I was in and out
of reality. Dazed (like I felt when I got my bell rung in college
intramural football: "Duh . . . yeah, I think I'm Max").

All day I felt as if I were in Oz or Disney World. I kept
waiting for a commercial to yank me back into reality. Silly

symptoms of love that I'd often thought foolish, I now experienced. Sweaty palms. Stuttering. Exuberance. Disbelief.

The day of the question. The question. She didn't know. At least I didn't tell her. (Turns out, however, that she expected it. She knew it was coming before I did.)

At T-minus-one-hour and counting, I prayed again as I was driving home from the jewelers (*the* jewelers, with *the* ring). "Lord, we're running out of time. If you don't want me to do it . . . wreck this van!" He didn't.

We had Chinese food at my apartment. The butterflies in my stomach weren't too hungry, so I didn't eat much. After dinner we sat on the couch. My arm hit a plant on the windowsill over our heads. It fell on top of her. Romantic, huh? Boy, I felt stupid.

We sat down to dessert. I had put my proposal in a fortune cookie. The world stopped as she began to read it. The angels stopped singing to listen. As she opened it, she began to cry. *Uh oh,* I worried, *I've done something wrong.*

But she said yes.

Had I the pen of a magician I couldn't describe my feelings at that moment. I was overwhelmed. Euphoric. Elated. Yet humbled that one so special could return my love. And grateful—that God would give me such a gift.

Does God have any part in the decisions and questions of your life?

Think about the gifts he's given you. Are you grateful to God? How can you live in gratitude?

43
FIVE VOTES OF CONFIDENCE

Today is a new day. Hence,

1. I refuse to be shackled by yesterday's failures.
2. What I don't know will no longer be an intimidation—it will be an opportunity.
3. I will not allow people to define my mood, method, image, or mission.
4. I will pursue a mission greater than myself by making at least one person happy they saw me.
5. I will have no time for self-pity, gossip, or negativism . . . from myself or from others.

What failures are you hanging on to, or even shackled by?

Do you allow people or circumstances to determine your attitudes and actions?

Whose mission do you pursue?

44
THE WEDDING
PRAYER

Create in us a love, O Lord.
  An eternal love . . .
  Your love.
  A love that forgives
       any failure,
    spans
       any distance,
    withstands
       any tempest.
Create in us a love, O Lord.
  A new love.
  A fresh love.
  A love with the tenderness
       of a lamb,
    the grandeur
       of a mountain,

the strength
of a lion.
And make us one. Intimately one.
As you made a hundred colors into one sunset,
A thousand cedars into one forest,
and countless stars into one galaxy . . .
make our two hearts as
one,

Father,
forever . . .
that you may be praised, Father,
forever.

If you are married, or planning to be, consider the prayer above.

Do you share the love of God?

Are you united in Christ?

What can you do today to pursue one united heart?

45
SARAH

Sarah sat alone. Her hands, freckled with age, rested in her lap. She wore her finest dress. Her nursing-home room spoke of springtime: daisies in the vase, a poinsettia blooming outside her window.

"Sundays are special, you know."

Her nursing-home wall spoke of family: an enlargement of grandson Jason hugging Brando the terrier; a framed portrait of her son Jerry, the dentist, and his family in Phoenix; Sarah and her late husband cutting their fortieth wedding anniversary cake. "It would have been fifty years next May."

Sarah sat alone. "They came last Christmas," she said brightly (as if defending her family).

A telegram and a birthday card were taped to the dresser mirror. A church group sang hymns down the hall. She had done her best to make the small room look homey, but a person can only do so much.

A thousand miles away a family played.

Sarah is not sick or ugly. She is not useless or decrepit. Sarah is simply old. Sarah is not senile, though at times, she confesses, the naïveté of senility is tempting. She doesn't suffer from cancer or arthritis. She hasn't had a stroke. No, her "disease" is much more severe. She suffers from rejection.

Our society has little room for the aged. People like Sarah come in scores. No one intentionally forgets them. Maybe that's why it is so painful. If there were a reason: a fight, a mistake, a dispute . . . But usually it's unintentional.

Unintentional rejection. It will kill Sarah; she'll die of loneliness. It doesn't matter how nice the convalescent home is; nurses and old folks don't replace a grandbaby's smile or a son's kiss.

Spend all your love on her now.
Forget not the hands, though spotted,
The hair, though thinning,
The eyes, though dim.
For they are a part of you.
And when they are gone, a part of you is gone.

Is there a convalescent in your acquaintance who needs your care today? What can you commit to doing on his or her behalf?

Who else is a part of you—your church body, your community, your workplace—who might need some kind of care, whether physical or emotional? What can you do to spend love on them?

Why should we care for the sick and aged and lonely? What does Jesus say about them?

46

THE SONAR FISH FINDER

I'm not one to complain about new inventions that make life easier. I love our toasters, hair dryers, calculators.

I think they make the little snags smoother in our day-to-day rituals. Yes, I like new ideas. . . . But this time we've gone a little bit far.

It's called the sonar fish finder, and it looks like a hair dryer. You put the nose end under the water and pull the trigger. A digital board responds to sensors on the nose, which in turn respond to the presence of fish. Gotcha! The poor little gilled creatures are victims of a radar system as advanced as anything used in World War II.

But the real loser isn't the fish. It's the fisherman.

I haven't done a lot in my life, but one thing I have done is fish. My father is hooked on fishing. In fact, I can't remember a single vacation during which we didn't fish. Our fishing was as consistent as Hank Aaron's bat. Hours on end. Riverbanks. Trout jumping. "Shhh, you'll scare the fish." Wet tennis shoes. Corks bobbing. Up early. Fifteen-horsepower motor. Minnows. Worms. Hooks. Stringers. Photographs. And man-to-man talks. (A fishing pole does wonders for conversation.) You name it, we talked about it. Football, girls, school . . . God. There's always time to talk when fishing.

You see, it never really matters if you catch any fish. Oh, sure, that's what everyone asks you: "What did you catch?" But the beauty of fishing is not in the catch—it's in the experience.

And a sonar fish finder? Well, it almost seems irreverent. It's like a do-it-yourself wedding or computerized dating. It's like electronic pitchers (dads are supposed to do *that,* too!) or those false logs you put in a fireplace.

Fishing is one of those sacred times that must not be violated and cannot be duplicated.

What is your sacred time? Afternoon walks with your friend? Early morning coffee with your wife? Long drives with your son? An afternoon at the beach with your daughter?

Maybe I'm making too big a deal about the fish finder. Then again, maybe not. The point is this: People are priceless. We should never allow a gadget to interfere with the precious simplicity of waiting for the fish to bite. If my father and I had bought a sonar fish finder, we'd have caught more fish, but countless precious conversations would have never existed.

My dad. The greatest fisherman in the world? Probably not. The greatest father? You'd better believe it.

Think about the special times in your life. Are you making time for them? Are you making time for the people in your life?

Whom do you value highly? Do they know it? Is it evident in the time you spend together?

Are any shortcuts, like the fish finder, cutting short the real experiences of your life?

47
TRIUMPHANT . . . FOREVER!

Triumph is a precious thing. We honor the triumphant. The gallant soldier sitting astride his steed. The determined explorer, returning from his discovery. The winning athlete holding aloft the triumphant trophy of victory. Yes, we love triumph.

Triumph brings with it a swell of purpose and meaning. When I'm triumphant, I'm worthy. When I'm triumphant, I count. When I'm triumphant, I'm significant.

Triumph is fleeting, though. Hardly does one taste victory before it is gone. Achieved, yet now history. No one remains champion forever. Time for yet another conquest, another victory. Perhaps this is the absurdity of Paul's claim: "But thanks be to God, who always leads us in triumphal procession" (2 Corinthians 2:14).

The triumph of Christ is not temporary. "Triumphant in Christ" is not an event or an occasion. It's not fleeting. To be triumphant in Christ is a lifestyle . . . a state of being!

To triumph in Christ is not something we do, it's something we are.

Here is the big difference between victory in Christ and victory in the world: A victor in the world rejoices over something he did—swimming the English Channel, climbing Everest, making a million. But the believer rejoices over who he is—a child of God, a forgiven sinner, an heir of eternity. As the hymn goes, "Heir of salvation, purchase of God, born of his Spirit, washed in his blood."

Nothing can separate us from our triumph in Christ. Nothing! Our triumph is based not upon our feelings but upon God's gift. Our triumph is based not upon our perfection but upon God's forgiveness. How precious is this triumph! For even though we are pressed on every side, the victory is still ours. Nothing can alter the loyalty of God.

A friend of mine recently lost his father to death. The faith of his father had for years served as an inspiration for many. In the moments alone with the body of his father, my friend said this thought kept coming to his mind as he looked at his daddy's face: *You won. You won. You won!* As Joan of Arc said when she was abandoned by those who should have stood by her, "It is better to be alone with God. His friendship will not fail me, nor his counsel, nor his love. In his strength I will dare and dare and dare until I die."

"Triumphant in Christ." It is not something we do. It's something we are.

Where do you find your significance? In your triumphs, or in Christ's?

What do you think it means to live in the triumphant lifestyle of Christ?

Do you know who you are in Christ? What implications does that have for the specific situations of your life: your relationships, your work, your leisure time, your daily reflections and worship?

48
THE MAKINGS OF
A MOVEMENT

Each of us should lead a life stirring enough to start a movement. We should yearn to change the world. We should love unquenchably, dream unfalteringly, and work unceasingly.

We should close our ears to the manifold voices of compromise and perch ourselves on the branch of truth. We should champion the value of people, proclaim the forgiveness of God, and claim the promise of heaven.

And we should lead a life stirring enough to cause a movement.

Will we see a movement occur? Perhaps, and perhaps not. Movements never run their course in one generation. The great revivals and reformations that dot the history of humanity were never the work of just one person. Every movement is the sum of visionaries who have gone before, generations of uncompromised lives and nonnegotiated truths. Faithful men who have led forceful lives.

Undoubtedly there have been many with Luther's

wisdom or Paul's oratory of whom we've heard nothing. Maybe an unknown butcher in Greece, a cobbler in France, a mechanic in Idaho. Men with godly lives that form a part of the foundation of a movement.

A movement comes of age when one life harvests the seeds planted by countless lives in previous generations. A movement occurs when one person, no greater or lesser than those who have gone before, lives a forceful life in the fullness of time. Never think that the great movements of Luther, Calvin, or Campbell were entirely of their own doing. They were simply forceful lives placed by God in a receptive crevice of history.

Let's live lives stirring and forceful enough to cause a movement. A true mark of the visionary is his willingness to lay down his life for those whom he'll never see.

Will that movement come in our generation? I hope so. But even if it doesn't, even if we never see it, it will occur. And we'll be a part of it.

What does the idea of a movement mean to you?

Is your life "stirring enough to cause a movement"? What kind of movement would that be?

How does God want you to live? What kind of choices must you make today in order to live as a follower of the ultimate Mover?

CONCLUSION

EMERGING FROM
THE ANVIL

49
OFF THE ANVIL

As I type the conclusion of this book, my thoughts are freshly stirred. My wife and I have just returned from an emergency trip to the United States to be with my father. He is very ill. He suffers from Lou Gehrig's disease, a muscle crippler for which there is no known cause or cure. We were called home, not knowing if he would be alive when we arrived. He was and still is. Yet, even though he has made significant improvement, we know, and he knows, that his time is nearing.

Dad is a man of extreme faith. An able teacher and a strong leader, he never left any doubt as to where he stood on the question of God. His first words to us as we saw him in the intensive care unit were "I'm ready to go to heaven. I think it's my time."

When the disease was first diagnosed, my wife and I were in the final stages of preparing to do mission work in Rio de Janeiro, Brazil. When I learned that Daddy had a terminal disease, I wrote him, volunteering to change my plans and stay near him. He immediately wrote back, saying, "Don't be concerned about me. I have no fear of death or eternity; just go . . . please him."

My father's life is an example of a heart melted in the fire of God, formed on his anvil, and used in his vineyard. He knew, and knows, what his life was for. In a society of question and confusion, his was one life that had a definition.

Time on God's anvil should do that for us: It should clarify our mission and define our purpose. When a tool emerges from a blacksmith's anvil, there is no question as to what it is for. There is no question as to why it was made. One look at the tool and you instantly know its function. You pick up a hammer and you know that it was made to hit nails. You pick up a saw and you know that it was made to cut wood. You see a screwdriver and you know that it is for tightening screws.

As a human being emerges from the anvil of God, the same should be true. Being tested by God reminds us that our function and task is to be about his business, that our purpose is to be an extension of his nature, an ambassador of his throne room, and a proclaimer of his message. We should exit the shop with no question as to why God made us. We know our purpose.

In a world of confused identity, in a world of wavering commitments and foggy futures, let us be firm in our role. Society is in dire need of a quorum of people whose task is clear and whose determination is unquenchable.

God has not hidden his will from his people. Our Master does not play games with us. We know who we are. We know what we are for. There may be a question now and then about how and with whom we should carry out his mission. But the underlying truth is still the same: We are God's people, and we are to be about his business.

If we live our lives in this way, then we can, like my father, enter into our final years with the assurance of knowing that life was well spent and that heaven is but a wink away.

And is there any greater reward than this?

Do you know your purpose, what you were made for? Whose business are you about: your own, or God's?

It's possible for even a longtime believer to live without a sense of purpose. Have you asked God to use your life for his service?

How do you think about eternity? Do you have any fear of death or the afterlife? Do you look forward to eternity with God?